LOVE THE LEAST OF MY CHILDREN

by

ELVIRA BELLEGONI

Drawings by

BETTY J. KOHLER

ETTA Publishing Company
Willowick, Ohio

LOVE THE LEAST OF MY CHILDREN

Published by:
ETTA Publishing Company
28605 Lakeshore Blvd.
Willowick, Ohio 44095

Printed in the United States of America
ISBN 0-9662542-4-4

To my spiritual homes: St. Wlliam Church, Euclid, Ohio and
St. Joseph Christian Life Center, Cleveland, Ohio

Elvira Bellegoni

To my Lord and Savior for He gave me the gift to draw.

Betty J. Kohler

PRAY

ENDURE

ACCEPT

CARE

EMPATHIZE

Autumn
or
Spring?
It does not
matter :
It lives !

SEEK GOD AND HE WILL COME

CLOSE YOUR EYES AND SEE THE LIGHT
BRING YOUR HEART TO THE LIGHT
AND FEEL THE WARMTH
GIVE HIM YOUR TEARS FOR HE
WILL CRY WITH YOU
BE FAITHFUL TO HIM
HE WILL BE WITH YOU FOREVER

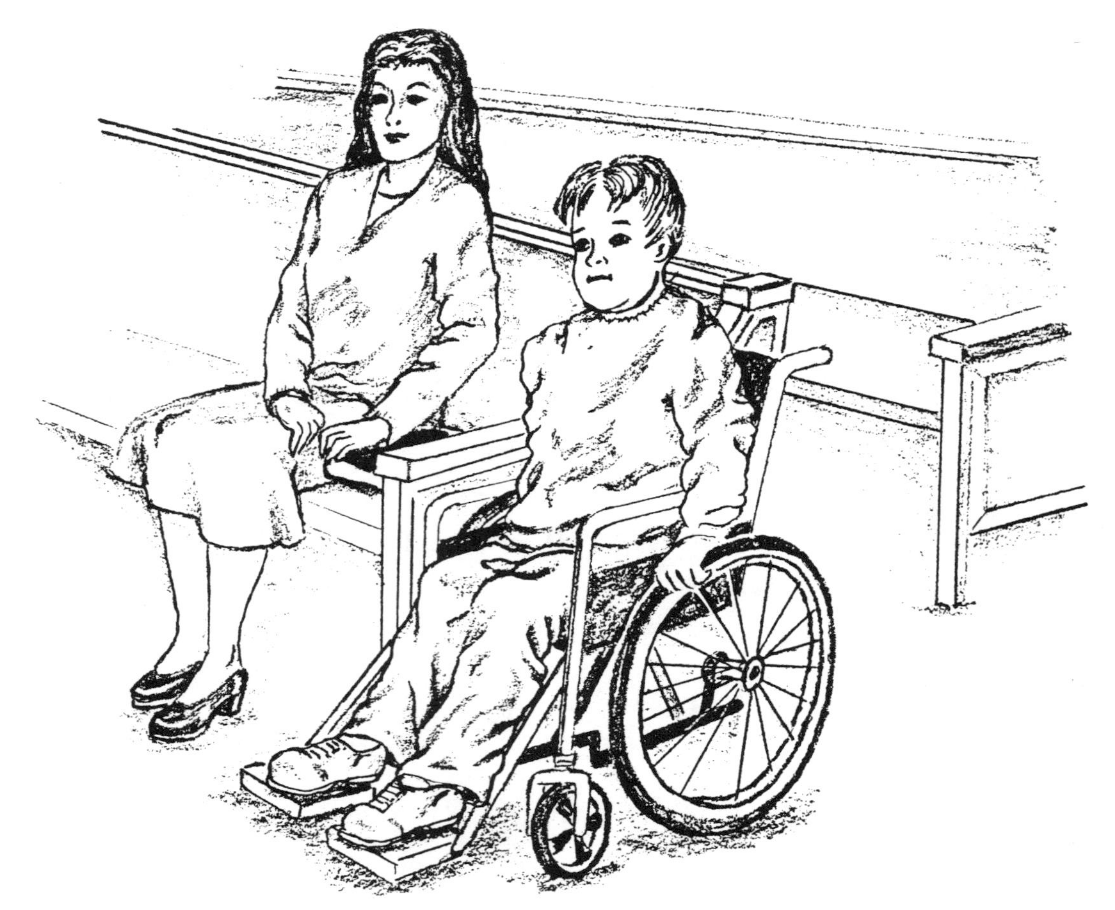

I have seen Jesus this morning.

*He looked at the handicapped child
and he looked at the people who passed
by pretending not to see him.*

He looked at his eyes screaming for love.

*He went to him, he touched him on the shoulder,
he smiled at him.*

I have seen Jesus this morning.

His name is Mark, he is ten years old.

HOLY
BIBLE

Best   Illustrated

Birth of Love

Everlasting

Why are her eyes so sad?

She sits in the same pew week after week, staring at a past.

Who is there in her mind? In her heart?

Her hands hold that rosary so tight.

Is the rosary a hand?

How I wish I could be next to her, her head on my shoulder,

my hand caressing her face.

I am sitting next to her

She has not looked at me.

Her eyes have not left the sight of her past.

I extend my hand, I touch her arm.

She pulls back, she still does not look at me.

God, help me to know what to do.

There she is. I sit next to her. I do not move.

I want to look at her, I want to touch her, but I do not move.

What does she think of me?

Can't she feel I really care for her?

She touches my hand and she whispers 'thank you'.

I cry.

Unlock the door,
Let GOD in

Footprints in the Sand

Never has such a poem spoken
so much truth in my heart.

Slowly going through my past,
I can see.

I can see You carrying me.
You carried me even when
I cursed You.

The stained glass is a picture of Jesus.

As I sit down and look at Him, His eyes are sad.

With my heart I pray for forgiveness and for His love.

I look up, His eyes are warm, a smile is now on His Face.

Seek GOD, He will come...

Sitting on a bench at the Christian Life Center,
surrounded by trees, plants, and flowers.
A sparrow lands on the bench table,
he chirps, and chirps, and chirps.
I chirp back and I tell him I love him.
I extend my hand ever so slowly,
he keeps chirping, only a few inches from my hand.
Again I tell him I love him,
I tell him I do not need to hold him in my hand,
he already is in my heart.
So gracefully he flies away.

Seek GOD, He will come.

Joy

Everlasting, only

Salvation

Under the

Stars

Heavens, Oceans, Spiritual Temple

THE SPARROW HE PROTECTS
THE DOVE IS HIS SON
THE SEED HE PUTS INTO FERTILE LAND
FAITH CAN GROW LIKE A SEED
THE SEED PUT ON A ROCK
THE ROCK WILL LET IT DIE
THE SEED ON THE ROCK PUT A CROWN
OF THORNS ON HIS HEAD

WARMTH:
>   the SUN, your EMBRACE

BEAUTY:
>   the SEA, your EYES

IMMENSITY:
>   The SKY, your LOVE

HOLD ME BY THE HAND.....

Without you I have eyes but I do not see,
I have legs but I do not move,
I have a heart but I do not feel..

HOLD ME BY THE HAND.

LOVE THE LEAST MY CHILDREN...

First I did not know,
When I knew I did not understand,
When I understood I did not believe.

Now I know, I understand, I believe.

When the mind and heart are as one:
I love You.

When the mind, the heart, and the soul are as one:
I know You love me, the least of Your children.

*8:30 a.m. ,Friday, the school children's mass.
I sit and I watch.*

*It is a beautiful sight: so many children,
so much love for God.*

*9:00 a.m., the mass has ended.
The church is empty,
the church is full of love.*

*I close my eyes and I see Jesus
touching the head of each child.*

Never alone am I. Oh, the warmth!

I sit on the floor by the stairwell and I close my eyes.

I call Him and He comes.

He embraces me from the back,
I can feel the warmth,
like a warm blanket.

GOD, you always come!

*I believe in angels. I met one today.
Unshaven face, shoddy cloths, shoes
too big for his feet.*

How long since he had a full meal?

He came over to me and he told me:

*'Don't look so sad, He loves you so much.
Give to Him your troubled heart,
He will fill it with joy.'*

Angels are beautiful!

God
Loves
You
The way you are

PRAY

ENDURE

ACCEPT

CARE

EMPATHIZE

I am home working in the garden.
The common flowers are so beautiful and so fragile.
A little sparrow lands on the fence chirping and
chirping.
I stop, I look at him, I smile.
Can he be the same sparrow as the one at the
Christian Life Center?
I get closer and closer.
He keeps chirping and chirping, jumping here
and there, an inch or two at the time, but he
does not fly away.
I am very close to him, he stays, I see glitter
in his eyes.
I close my eyes and I say: 'Thank you God for
the beauty You put in my life.'
I open my eyes, the sparrow is gone.

Is this true love? It must be!

Never have I felt such a great understanding,
so great that the pain twists the pit of my
stomach.

Do I truly, finally, love her? It must be!

I feel such great pain for her, for her pain:

How could she bear to see her son suffer
and die as He did?

Amazing   Love,

Torch

Almighty   Radiant

...THIS IS MY BODY...THIS IS MY BLOOD.

Oh, forgive me, forgive me Lord.

How unfit I am of your love and still you love me.

How far could I be like your disciples?

How soon would I give up?

How unfit I am of your love and still you love me.

Thou shalt have no other
Gods before me
Thou shalt not make
unto thee any graven
images
Thou shalt not take the
Lord thy God in vain
Remember the sabbath
to keep it Holy
Honor thy father
and thy mother

Thou shalt not kill
Thou shalt not
Commit adultery
Thou shalt not steal
Thou shalt not bear
false witness against
thy neighbor
Thou shalt not covet
thy neighbors wife
nor anything that is
thy neighbors

GOOD

ORDERLY

DIRECTION

$$C_{OMFORTING,}$$

$$U_{NCONDITIONAL}$$

$$P_{IETY}$$

*Time to get beautiful! I shall wear my best
dress, make-up and hair looking perfect.
I will go to my rendezvous with him with a
trepidant heart.
I have refused at times to go meet him,
but he always has come,
he always has waited for me.
What a great love!
Here I am, I have arrived. With blessed water
I sign myself, I kneel:
Thank you GOD for always welcoming me
in your home.
Help me to make my inside as clean and
as nice as my outside.*

PEACE
AND
LOVE
OIL

The Time
is Always
Right

About the author:

Elvira Bellegoni has written extensively through the years. Some of her publications are: *'Wanted: A Home. Very Abused Kitten Needs a Home Desperately'*, ($13.95) *'Bookkeeping and Administration for the Smaller Business'* ($12.95), and *'Parliamo Italiano'* (which includes a 60 minutes audio cassette) ($14.95.)
Elvira is in the process of writing her next book, *'What do you mean I am 50?'* (Humor, spirituality, reality check.)

About the illustrator:

Betty J. Kohler has been drawing for many years. Spiritual themes and animals are her favorite subjects. She has illustrated the book *'Wanted: A Home. Very Abused Kitten Needs a Home Desperately'*.

A message from ETTA Publishing Company :

We truly hope this book has brought you added peace and closeness to God.

We are looking for people who would like to participate in the writing of our next book: *'Of God and Angels'*. The book will be a collection of poems/short writings about feelings, experiences, and thoughts about God and Angels. If we publish your writing, your name, your city, and your state will appear at the end of the writing.

Send your writing to:

ETTA Publishing Company
28605 Lakeshore Blvd.
Willowick, Ohio 44095

ORDER FORM

Name of book ____

Price per book ______________X quantity ordered ____ = _______________

Shipping & Handling (see below)   _______________

Total   _______________
Shipping & Handling:
First book, $2.50, any additional book
add $.60.

Mail the order form and your check to: ETTA Publishing Company
28605 Lakeshore Blvd.
Willowick, Ohio 44095

Your name and address ___________________________________

____